D0381233

The Enigma of
Al Capp

FANTAGRAPHICS BOOKS
7563 Lake City Way NE
Seattle, WA 98115

Published by Gary Groth & Kim Thompson
Edited by Ilse Thompson
Art Director: Carrie Whitney

First Fantagraphics Books edition: January 1999

ISBN: 1-56097-340-4

Printed in Canada

The Enigma of
Al Capp

by Alexander Theroux

FANTAGRAPHICS BOOKS

Satire was his gift, and with its ancillary weapons of burlesque and parody, Al Capp needed nothing more to become, with his *Li'l Abner*, in the opinion of many, America's greatest comic strip, one of this country's icons for more than half a century. "I think Capp may very possibly be the best writer in the world today," wrote novelist John Steinbeck in 1952, who also regarded him as "the best satirist since Laurence Sterne." It was his judgment that Capp "has not only invented a language but has planted it in us so deeply that we can talk it ourselves." His was an art of national force. "Not very many of our institutions and states of mind have escaped Capp. No other writer that I know has created folklore as he goes along and made it stick.... I can think of only Cervantes and Rabelais who have succeeded in doing this before Capp." Steinbeck concluded that if the Nobel Prize committee was at all alert, it should seriously have considered this artist.

He was also a man of great complexity, of reckless, even dangerous extremes. His was a life touched by early tragedy, a setback which, although overcome by creative transformations of a unique kind, led him through caricature and cartoons into other worlds with which he seemed unable to deal and that even the black humor of his art either couldn't save or wouldn't spare. Who exactly was Al Capp? More than anyone, he cannot be summed up in a few words.

Al Capp—né Alfred Gerald Caplin (1909-1979)—was born on September 28 on Stevens Street, New Haven, Connecticut, in a house in a benighted section of town he often called a "ghetto." Shortening his name to Capp (he commonly referred to it as his "maiden name") when he first began signing his comic strip, he had it legally changed in 1949. The growing family was rather poor. He had two younger brothers, Jerome and Elliott, and a sister, Madeleine, who later became a press agent. (One of her principal accounts was her brother.) Jerome was for a while general manager of Capp Enterprises, Inc., a thriving corporation that sold *Li'l Abner*-related toys, comic books, costume jewelry, even ladies' blouses. Elliott had also been a comic strip author and wrote the continuity for a syndicated strip called *Dr. Bobbs*. Otto, the father, was a feckless schemer and bankrupt who lost job after job and shifted the family about constantly. He ended up a salesman of industrial oil. He had artistic ability himself, according to Al. Both his father and his mother, Tillie, born a Samuelson—at one time her father had been Grand Rabbi of New York City—were natives of Latvia and had immigrated to America when they were children.

When Capp was eleven, the family moved to the Brownsville (or, as he put it, "Murder, Inc.") section of Brooklyn, and then was shunted back to Bridgeport, Connecticut, where Al attended Central High School, though, curiously, he never graduated either because he couldn't—or wouldn't—pass a required course in geometry. (He believes he set a world's record by flunking that subject nine straight terms.) Al began drawing cartoons in grade school and even then was selling copies to the neighborhood children. As a boy, he read that Billy DeBeck was making a fortune with his creation of *Barney Google* and that Bud Fisher, of *Mutt and Jeff* fame, had married a countess. He decided to become a cartoonist ("I knew... cartooning was not just a trick but a step beyond illustration," he later said, "a kind of illustration of your own point of view") and, after going to Boston at 19, went to Philadelphia, spent not quite a year studying art there, then returned to Boston. He never managed to take a degree, though he would succeed beyond his wildest dreams at what he had eventually set out to do, at the top of his form, earning more than $500,000 a year from his strip and its numerous spin-offs, including a Broadway musical and two movies. In a remarkably short time he became a wealthy man.

He was a self-made man, ambitious, witty, and extremely outgoing. He smoked all his life (Benson & Hedges, which his secretary, Millie Maffei, bought by the carton from DeLuca's on Charles Street) and wolfed Tums regularly for a gippy tummy that never settled. "Get me a bicarb!" he'd bellow constantly from his seat at the drawing board and drank five or six of them a day. He drank nothing else. He hated alcohol and called himself a "chronic non-alcoholic." He loved borscht, kept

jars of it in a refrigerator at work, and slopped it all the way back to his drawing board. Though he became a millionaire, he often said he thought he was broke. His grandchildren—Caitlin and Tamsin, Julie's daughters, and Willie, Cathie's son—called him "Gumpy," which was also his code name. Al disliked animals, though there was a studio cat, "Eartha Cat," that managed to live on premises for a while. ("I'd like to put two pieces of bread around her and make a sangwich," Capp often grumped.) Also, a dog named Clay hung around, a big black Labrador named, pejoratively, after Muhammed Ali, with whom Al, especially during the Vietnam era, when the boxer famously refused to be drafted into the Army, came to have small sympathy.

And he was something of a flaneur. He wore blue banker's suits from Saville Row with silk handkerchiefs in his vest pockets and Chesterfield coats and drove a maroon Buick convertible. He always made it a point to dress well and often referred to himself as the "Patent-leather Yid." John Lobb was his London boot maker. "Dress British; think Yiddish," he used to say. He had no use for humility. He had dyed his hair black for decades to hide the gray. "I think of myself as a Jewish Cary Grant," he was given to boast. He was a distinct Anglophile. He adored the Savoy Hotel in London, where he always stayed ("From the instant you enter it, you are not merely the guest of the hotel, you are the cherished charge of several hundred of the greatest diplomats Britain has ever produced, working as bellhops, porters, waiters, clerks, whose one desire in life, clearly, is to make you happy.... There's nothing on earth like the Savoy, nothing as splendid....")

Capp met his future wife, Catherine Wingate Cameron, in art school in Boston. He gave us a brief and

witty autobiographical account of their meeting and subsequent marriage in a comic strip, which he drew in
booklet form in 1946 for the benefit of veteran World
War II amputees, called "Al Capp by Li'l Abner," a piece
included in his memoirs, *My Well-Balanced Life on a
Wooden Leg* (John Daniel & Company, 1991), essays
compiled and published years after his death. Catherine,
who was twenty-one when she married Capp, had black
hair, big blue eyes, and lived with her parents in
Amesbury, Massachusetts. She continued to live there
after their marriage while her almost penniless husband
sought his fortune in New York. (After Al died, she married again.) The inspiration and model for the
enchantress Moonbeam McSwine, she became his first
assistant and worked for a while on *Li'l Abner*, doing
backgrounds and lettering for the strip. It is Catherine
we can thank for naming Daisy Mae and Pansy Yokum.
Al and Catherine had two natural daughters and one
adopted boy, Colin ("Kim"). Julie was the older of the
three; Catherine ("Cathie"), an Ophelia like girl, five
years her junior, who married Michael Pierce, a photog-
rapher, but whose brief and troubled young life sudden-
ly ended when, after a long
period of despondence, she
committed suicide.

    The Capps lived on
Brattle Street, Cambridge,
Massachusetts, in a large old
house presided over by their
beautiful black maid, Dicey, a
soft-spoken woman with whom
Mrs. Capp would often go to
the movies. The Capps also
owned a sixty-five acre farm in
South Hampton, New
Hampshire. (A restless man,

especially toward the end of his life, Capp also owned a Park Avenue, New York apartment—Millie often had to go there and "straighten up New York.") The actual studio in Boston where the strip was done was located on the top floor of a prim little brick apartment building on 122 Beacon Street, exactly next to Emerson College. (Capp had done his drawings for a while, in the thirties, in a studio in Ball Square, Somerville.) Other working rooms were on the spare first floor, where there was a den, one enormous front room, a long hall, and a living room area that overlooked the Charles River. It was his sanctuary, where he worked. He needed work, and above all, the strip. It was the comic strip alone that gave Al Capp his sole identity, and, perhaps, maybe his only reason for living. His strip, in a way, *was* stripping: a means of showing off, for a kid who grew up crippled with diffidence and rendered almost immobile with thoughts of self-doubt and fear.

At nine years old, on August 21, 1919, in an agonizing moment that in a very real sense never ended—one he referred to as "the nightmare of my life"—Al Capp lost a leg. On his way to get a haircut, hoping to save money by going across town to a cheaper barber shop in New Haven, he tried hitching a ride on an ice truck, slipped off, and a trolley car ran over his leg. Unconscious, he was found, even in the hospital, clutching in his small fist the 50-cent piece, which his mother, out of pain or remorse, saved for years but, Al noted somewhere, eventually spent during the Depression. (For all the autobiographical matter he wrote, Capp is curiously silent about his mother.) His left leg had to be amputated well above the knee. He felt like Ahab himself, "unmanned." "It was an age of Whiteness," he recorded later, "A white bed, white-clad nurses, white-clad doctors, shining white instruments—white—a horrible, ghastly age of Whiteness." We are given a comic strip account of the tragedy in the booklet Capp later drew for veteran amputees, which of course necessarily diminishes the extent of the trouble and pain Capp faced as a result of the lost leg. This version of how Capp lost his leg may be passingly apocryphal. It was the explanation he gave to *Life* magazine, but Dave Schreiner writes, "It is possible that the story of the coin is not true; the usual explanation is that he jumped the wagon to snatch a shard of ice on a hot day, then fell off," which would be considerably less romantic. One suspects we have to be skeptical of many things that Capp has said.

He limped. He fell frequently. He looked ridiculous, he thought. He felt awkward, often ashamed, with girls—something, one suspects, he never came to terms with—and was given to odd ruses, tricks, and pathetic strategies, to avoid being seen and, at least so he surmised, mocked. The psychological damage to Capp probably never healed. Capp, in a very real sense, never really felt like a normal person. I once saw him, in the summer of 1964, walking through the Boston Arts Festival. He veered and bobbed: one leg dragged, the

other dipped. At every other step, he flung his left leg forward, as if, like ballast, it were bringing the right forward, a gait that gave out a squeak as the left leg fell. (For a while it was fastened cumbersomely to a harness over the shoulder.) Capp often said, with a strain of wistfulness in the false cheer, "I walk like Long John Silver." He could never stay on upper floors in hotels and often had to be driven places, taken in carts through airports, and so forth. The "leg repair shop," where Millie once, very grudgingly, certainly squeamishly, had to bring the leg in a brown paper bag, "to get bolts," was a prosthetics center—Al always said the world sounded obscene—ironically named J. E. Hanger of New England, Inc., 804 Huntington Avenue, Boston, Massachusetts. And what do we make of the fact that his wooden leg was actually made by guy named Butcher? Who more than Capp would have felt the full thump of that?

As John Updike has observed in an introduction to the posthumously published memoirs, losing his leg

left Capp in "permanent banishment from the paradise of the normal." It became the central fact of his life. "I really don't think it's a joke," Capp wrote. "It's quite an inconvenience." Updike astutely went on to observe, "The ebullient, at times raunchy exaggeration of bodies that is one of Dogpatch's striking features related, surely, to the somatic awareness induced by Capp's missing limb and

its painful, awkward substitute." Reading over Al Capp's stories, essays, and articles, one can't help but notice that he had girls, sex, and seduction almost always on his mind, and the feelings of inferiority he felt in the face of it all, growing up with a missing leg and a limp—forcing him, in order to look normal, into stratagems and subterfuges—are painful to read, simply because he was so self-conscious. His wooden leg squeaked, fell apart, and got stuck constantly. "As long as I stayed in one place, the girls I stared at and whistled at treated me like any other street-corner wise guy" Capp wrote. A brief piece in the memoirs, "Short Skirts," as Updike notes, is ostensibly about sex, but is "virtually about legs." Steps and stairs. Stairs and steps. Taking them, in pulls and stops, is "the only experience with my wooden leg," Capp confessed even years later, "that irritates me to this day. When I was a boy, it was a humiliation I'd go to any length to avoid."

But a life he had to live. Capp went to New York early in 1932 to find work, after deciding early to become a cartoonist. "I heard that Bud Fisher (creator of *Mutt 'n Jeff*) got $3,000 a week and was constantly marrying

French countesses," Capp recalled. "I decided that was for me." He kicked around, living in airless rat-hole rooms in Greenwich Village, reading menus in the windows of restaurants until he found a place he could afford. He was "mouse poor," as Milton Caniff recalled. It was soon arranged through his uncle, Harry Resnick, that someone at Associated Press would look at his drawings. Wilson Hicks, an editor, liked the work and offered Capp $52 a week to draw a single-frame strip called *Colonel Gilfeather*, a rather pale and derivative imitation of *Major Hoople*. Capp hated doing someone else's strip. After six months, he was replaced by an apprentice artist there, Caniff himself, a friend whose work he came to admire. Meanwhile, Capp, who also assisted Rube Goldberg during those early days, got another job in 1933. Hammond Fisher, creator of the immensely successful *Joe Palooka*, hired him to finish a Sunday page for $10. It was to become a controversial relationship.

Capp worked briefly as Fisher's full-time assistant at $22.50 a week—later, creatively, Fearless Fosdick's petty salary, when he was paid at all—working

on *Joe Palooka* and living pretty much hand to mouth in a cellar apartment. It was in this strip that Capp first drew the hillbilly characters, inserting them into the strip while his boss was on vacation, that Fisher would later claim Al plagiarized. The two men were soon feuding. Capp felt he had been underpaid and unappreciated, and Fisher not only accused Capp of stealing Li'l Abner's body but for giving him the very same attributes that made big, dumb, innocent, sentimental Joe Palooka famous, along with the effusion of traditional values and glories of the simple life that the congenial boob of boxing had come to personify. A rivalry was one thing; now a war began. When Fisher had his nose redone, Capp maliciously put a horse named "Ham's Nose-Bob" into his own strip. Capp also wrote an essay called "I Remember Monster" for the *Atlantic Monthly* (May 1951) in which he savagely dissed Fisher, though never mentioning him by name. There was litigation.

The full conflict broke into print in *Time* on February 14, 1955, when that magazine reported that Ham Fisher had accused Capp of putting pornographic material into *Li'l Abner*—an accusation that came just as Capp and some associates were trying to buy a Boston television station. Capp responded to his former boss' charges by calling Fisher a "treasure trove of lousiness who, in the normal course of each day of his life, managed to be, in dazzling succession, every conceivable kind of heel." Within weeks after the *Time* article, the 325-member National Cartoonists Society suspended Fisher for "conduct unbecoming a member." He was in turn accused of using "altered... tampered-with... and not a true reproduction" of Capp's cartoons in an effort to prove Capp had slipped pornography into his drawings. A few months later, on December 27, 1955, Fisher in despair, committed suicide by taking an overdose of sleeping pills. He had been dying of cancer at the time, but the contretemps with Capp must have weighed heavily on him as well.

Subsequent to that apprenticeship, Capp spent less than a year working in New York before United Features finally came to see the potential of *Li'l Abner*, a strip that, although it had metamorphosed down through the years, most notably going from adventure stories to a strip of semi-sophisticated satire—Al's vehicle for social criticism, as a matter of fact—kept up such a high quality in regard to both running text and drawing for almost half a century that it would be later described by Alain Resnais, that most revered of Nouvella Vague French film directors, as "America's one immortal myth and the dominating artistic influence of my life."

Li'l Abner made its first appearance in the *New York Daily Mirror* on August 13, 1934, the same year as Otto Soglow's *The Little King*, Milton Caniff's *Terry and the Pirates*, Alex Raymond's *Flash Gordon*, and Fred Lasswell's *Barney Google and Snuffy Smith*. It was also the year of the first Thurber cartoons in *The New Yorker*. It was the age of comics—comic strips and comic books, a specific literary genre and art form, one I've always thought aligned to its close cousin, early radio, where dramas and episodes took the place of cartoon-like characters like The Shadow, Sergeant Preston of the Yukon, Boston Blackie, The Lone Ranger, The Green Hornet, Jack Armstrong the All American Boy, and Mr. Keen: Tracer of Lost Persons. The fact was, comics were even more popular. In a critical essay on comics that Capp wrote in 1946 for a four-volume supplement to the *Encyclopedia Britannica*, he noted, "The comic strip during the decade 1937 to 1946 became, in terms of the constancy of the devotion of its followers, the most popular U.S. entertainment, surpassing radio and the motion picture."

Capp's comic strip would last 43 years. It was the first humorous strip to attempt serious political satire, as well as the very first in a sort of metafictional way to parody other comic strips, and, all in all, was virtually an instant success, appearing in roughly 900 newspapers by the late 1960s. (Al gained full control of the strip gradually, aided by a highly celebrated lawsuit against his syndicate in the mid-1940s.) At its pinnacle, Capp and his cartoon strip would eventually reach as many as 90 million people a day. "More Americans give me a piece of their day," Al Capp could boast in 1946, "than anyone else in the whole country." And he was as faithful as his fans. Julie, his eldest daughter, later reflected, "My father's favorite way to begin a family dinner conversation was to say, 'Wait until I tell you what happened to Abner today!' He would then proceed, with each Gulp! and Haw Haw! and Bop! and Chomp! in the script, to tell us the latest adventures of the Yokums and other denizens of Dogpatch. We always knew, even as the tiniest of children, the right moment to laugh—because he always laughed first." And he had a raucous laugh, indeed.

Al had a particular fondness for Chaplin and in fact once wrote an essay on the famous comedian ("The Comedy of Charles Chaplin"). For anyone whose profession is visual comedy," Capp wrote, "it is necessary to study the work of Charlie Chaplin as it is for an engineer to study mathematics." It was Chaplin's *ineptness*, Capp felt, that endeared him to us. Abner would also be inept. "In my work... I have tried to make cheerier a world of disappointed lovers. No lover is anything but disappointed, since the greatest of all disappointments is the final triumphant possession of the love one has dreamed of having. It's never as wonderful as your dreams of it, because there are no limits to the wonderfulness of dreaming."

He always loved and admired "the great funny guys," especially his favorites, Fred Opper, Milt Gross, Maurice Ketlen, Cliff Sterrett, Rudy Dirks, who did *The*

Katzenjammer Kids (based on Wilhelm Busch's *Max and Maurice*, which was first published in comic book form in 1870). He had a special fondness for the great Rube Goldberg, in whose memory are awarded "Reubens," the Oscars of cartooning. Al won one in 1947. Cruikshank, Hogarth, Daumier, and George Herriman were also his heroes. He loved *Krazy Kat*, the seminal strip that went from 1911 to 1944, the year Herriman died. He also admired *Pogo* and Walt Kelly. There were rivalries among cartoonists, of course, but mostly innocent fun when they could lampoon each other. At one point in his strip, for example, Capp satirized Mary Worth with her horrifying perfection—as Mary Worm—where she became a big-breasted, bromide-spouting meddler. An answering satire followed in *Mary Worth* ridiculing "Hal Rapp," a man with a gross, distended lower lip. Capp said the feud was a hoax, that he and Allen Saunders (writer) and Ken Ernst (cartoonist) were the best of friends, and that Rapp would turn out to be a good fellow.

Capp always drew the cartoon himself; no one else. "No matter what else happens to me, I'm God himself when I sit down at this drawing board." Very early, he used tricks to lure the eyes of readers away from strips which ran below and above his own, making his figures big and simple, and clothed in black whenever possible. His characters screamed things in bold face: "Ah is gonna give yo' a bath once a month," Mammy Yokum tells Pappy, "whether yo' needs it or **NOT**!!" He used to great advantage the Ben Day printing process, a technique of shading using dots, as Seurat had, which was invented by Benjamin Day (1836-1916). He was a matchless master of the human face and made the funniest ones ever. No caricature hasn't been done in *Li'l Abner*, an elaborate funny farm of goofy eyes, odd clothes, huge chins, elongated heads, jutting ears, peculiar hairstyles, a whole range of noses, and especially profiles. The profile sums up the essence of a subject, as caricaturists are well aware when they wish to capture a personality. *Li'l Abner* always also had a large amount of dialog. And Al loved exclamation marks, and often used two!! He also employed expletives to great advantage, especially favorites like "thud," "groan," "sob!" He also used to great effect Jewish words and locutions, with much "victim" humor employed. (Shmoo=schmo? Schmuck?) Food always played a big part in the strip. And sex. Capp kept a small round mirror affixed to his drawing board, exactly as Charles Dickens in his day did, in order to practice a whole array of rubbery comic faces and get them right.

Al was lucky to have two brilliant assistants, Andy Amato and Harvey Curtis. (In the early fifties, Walter Johnston was Capp's other assistant, before Harvey Curtis, who was younger than the others, came aboard. And Stan Lee, later of Marvel Comics, and Bob Lubbers, who did *The Heart of Juliet Jones*, both once worked for Capp, as did Frank Frazetta, who later became very popular in his own right.) Andy Amato was a first-rate cartoonist, lived with his mother, smoked cigars, and died in the mid-70s. (At the wake, when he was laid out at Dello Russo's funeral home in Medford, Massachusetts, Harvey dryly commented, "There should be a cigar in his hand instead of a rosary.") Andy, like Al, had never finished art school. Both Curtis and Andy were very quiet and standoffish, but it was Andy who was "the real nut," according to secretary Millie Maffei, "who came up with so many great ideas, and it was Andy who did the background figures and who drew in many of the little additions that made the strip so great." Harvey Curtis, who looked like a little accountant, a sort of Mr. Peepers, was very prim, lived alone, had a gun collection, and also collected antique cars. Al, who drove from Brattle Street, Cambridge to Boston every day—eventually he hired a chauffeur—usually breezed into work, muttering "Ah hoo ha," his way of saying hello to everybody.

All worked together in the studio rooms on Beacon Street. Six "dailies" a week were required, six to eight weeks ahead of time. After Al and Andy and Harvey got together, laughing and howling behind closed doors during "story sessions" as they came up with a week's worth of fable, dialog, and ideas—always written down by Capp in pencil on green-lined steno pads in the exclusive language of Dogpatch—they'd then adjourn to their respective drawing boards. (At work, all three for their own amusement spoke Li'l Abnerese, nacherly, like "Ah's hongry" or "Thass a fack" or "Thar's never an idiot around when yo' needs one!") Preliminary drawings followed. Al and Andy did this mostly, roughing out the action of the strip in pencil. Al inked the heads and bodies of the main characters, getting the "look" of each strip. Andy did most of the other inking. Harvey cut the boards, lined the strip, applied the Ben Days, did the lettering and whatever white-outs were necessary. He also signed all the strips and did the Sunday strip coloring.

The team generally took about four hours to do a daily strip, around ten to do a Sunday one for the multicolor supplement, which took longer to print. Working in bursts of energy, Capp was generally able to produce a couple of weeks' material in four or five days, making sure, for suspense, the story-line of the strip always ended on Wednesday. "If I ended one on a Saturday," he often repeated, "millions of my readers would have nothing to worry about over the weekend and would forget me and turn to *Popeye*." He was a driven man. He never wasted any time, even traveling. He always carried looseleaf notebooks to write down ideas, names, plots, compose dialog, even do sketches. He'd come back from trips—part of his secretary's job was to empty his jackets—his pockets stuffed with papers, notes for speeches, checks for thousands of dollars, and piles and piles of empty Tums wrappers. He loved to scream to his secretary, "Millie, take a letter! Come in with your notepad! Now!" and begin firing away. "Mr. Capp, I'm sorry, but I don't do shorthand." "What!! And you told me—" And Millie would sigh, "I do every time." It was a variation of an act they always went through for laughs, "Big Boss" and "Ruby Keeler."

When finished strips were ready to mail, Millie took the brown rectangular envelopes ("Newspaper Matrices/Do Not Bend") around the corner to the lobby of the Ritz Carlton Hotel, shot them down the slide, and they were off to the C.T.N.Y.N.S., the syndicate, that is the great central castle of the cartoon world, where it all came together, the Chicago Tribune-New York News Syndicate, 220 East 42nd Street, New York, New York 10017.

It is of course the Yokums of *Li'l Abner* who take our main attention: Mammy (Pansy), a small, pipe-smoking runt, "undisputed champeen sassiety leeder of Dogpatch," who always marked her forehead with a bloody cross and whirled around three times to see visions; Pappy (Lucifer), her little weakling of a husband (he is 4'4"; she is 4'5") who frequently needs to be washed in a hopper, whose trousers she irons while he is wearing them, and who can sniff out gold after eating messes of "presarved tarnips." Tiny, Abner's fifteen-and-a-half year old brother; Salomey the family pig, who is def-

THE LI'L VARMINT GOT A SMUG LOOK ON HIS LI'L FACE, NOW THET HE'S DISCOVERED HE IS KING OF THE SKONKS —

12-9

initely a Yokum; and last but not least there is Li'l Abner himself—dumb, handsome, young (he remains 19 years old today, just as he was in 1934), slow, patriotic, naive, but like Candide, a person who exposes human folly, greed and stupidity wherever he goes. ("When Li'l Abner speaks," said Capp, "he speaks for millions of morons.") A character said to be based on many people, among them Henry Fonda,

Henry Wallace, and young Al Capp himself, he is governed by his iron fisted mother, loves to dip pork chops in tea, and stoutly defends the "Yoo Ess Ay" under any and all circumstances. His jeans always have two knee patches, one striped, one dotted. His hair is always parted on the side nearest to the viewer. And after years of being pursued by beautiful girls, he was finally caught by, and so married, the voluptuous Daisy Mae, by whom he had a son, Honest Abe. The Yokums, who live in a one-room shack with an outhouse and subsist on a diet of turnips and pork chops, live a life neither hygienic nor hopeful.

Dogpatch, their hamlet—"an average stone-age community," as Capp described it—is a hill-bound heartland that has been variously situated in a deep valley, on a desert beside a high mountain ("Onnecessary Mountain"), and on top of that very same peak. (There is a theme park outside of Harrison, Arkansas called Dogpatch!) It is a place with as many legends and locations as Trollope's Barchester or Faulkner's Yoknapatawpha. West Po'kchop Railroad, which is owned by Idiot J. Tolliver, runs almost perpendicularly up one side of Onnecessary Mountain and then straight down the other. (J. R. Fatback, the hog tycoon, once ordered that the mountain be tilted sideways with enormous jacks to keep its shadow from falling on his breakfast egg.) There's also Kissing Rock, which is handy to Suicide Cliff; Ole Man Mose's Cave; the Skonk Works, a smelly place, where skonk oil is brewed and barreled by its proprietor, Big Barnsmell and his "outside" man, Barney Barnsmell. We learn from the comic strip autobiography of 1946, done for fellow amputees, that young Capp actually did once travel South before inventing Li'l Abner. And he even claimed he had once met Li'l Abner's prototype in person. There was actually a character, a small lad, named Abner in the *Gilfeather* strip of the early thirties. And Julie Capp Cairol later acknowledged that, if she had been born a boy, I was to be called 'Abner' by my parents."

All the goons and grotesques of *Li'l Abner*, all the villains, shysters, hucksters, pea-and-thimble riggers, the full range, as John Dryden said of Chaucer's pilgrims, of "God's Plenty," are children of that strip: Cousin Weakeyes; Available Jones, factotum and a man open for anything ("Babies Watched, dry babies five cents, wet babies ten cents"); Joe Btfsplk, "the world's most loving friend and worst jinx," with his perpetual cloud raining down bad luck on everyone (In a 1940 Sunday page, Joe Btfsplk announces to Abner that he is off to see "...a fella which needs me. Fella named Adolf"); the speedy McZip Brothers; Miss Prudence Pimpleton, Fearless Fosdick's gnathic fiancee (an engagement of seventeen years!) whose jutting jaw perfectly resembled his own; Hairless Joe and his faithful little bulb-nosed Indian sidekick, Lonesome Polecat, who dispensed hair-curling batches of Kickapoo Joy Juice; Lena the Hyena, the world's ugliest woman; Evil-Eye Fleegle, zoot suited master of the "triple whammy"; the terrible Nightmare Alice and her little Dogpatch voodoo dolls; Senator Phogbound, with his windy broken promises; Eddie Ricketyback; Bet-a-Million Bashby; Flash Manglebugle, the world's greatest promoter; fat, gluttonous Bounder J. Roundheels, who had wanted to join "Gourmet's Club" since 1909. finally gets elected, but is then eaten as he in fact *becomes* the "ecstasy sauce" he craved; Earthquake McGoon, and hundreds more. Only occasionally did Capp become a bit obvious and hamhanded in his Rabelaisian choice of names for that long parade of vaudeville hillbillies, with

tags like Clamwinkle McSlop, Wanda Meatball, and Dave Dogmeat. And how about the Atom Bum?

But who can forget the Abominable Snow-Hams, who smell like the finest roast ham? Or the Kigmies, who love to be kicked (until they learn to love kicking *back*)? Or any of the wonderful Bald Iggles; the Hammus Alabamus, Salomey, the Yokum family pig; Fried Dog Indians, who have never surrendered to the USA, or Native American Kickapoos—*Newsweek* (February 22, 1965), with Capp's blessing, announced Kickapoo Joy Juice was currently available in supermarkets and in the sixties there was a 45 r.p.m. record by the Rivingtons called "Kickapoo Joy Juice" (Liberty)? Dogpatch Hams, amazingly, can regenerate themselves after you take off a

slice. (Jewish Capp—will it be a dissertation subject one day?—seems to have had a strange and recurrent fixation about that meat.) And how about the inimitable Shmoos, those gentle, hybrid, penis-shaped creatures who lay large pre-packaged eggs, give grade A bottled milk, neatly wrapped quarter pounds of butter, and even, occasionally, cheesecake? What's more, at the sight of a hungry human being, the solicitous little beasts will roll over and die of joy, whereupon, when fried, they taste like chicken, when broiled, like steak. Their bodies can be also used for lumber (when cut thick) or leather (when cut thin), their whiskers as perfect toothpicks! These characters, who became a national craze in 1949, led to more than a hundred marketable Shmoo-inspired items, such as cottage cheese in Shmoo jars, Shmoo pencils, Shmoo balloons, Shmoo notebooks, and no end of Shmooiana, including Shmoo cocktails, Shmooveralls, and Shmoo toys. There was even a Shmoo rhumba going around.

"The beasts never occurred to me in any other form," Al Capp told *The New Yorker* in 1964—also illustrating his liberal thoughts at the time—of the fat little creatures who climbed out of a crater near Dogpatch and began to reproduce with cheerful proliferation. "And as soon as I drew the first Shmoo, I knew what its name was going to be. What did trouble me was speaking through Shmoos at all. McCarthy was coming to power when I created Shmoos, and those were inconceivably terrible times. They got worse and worse, until eventually the only satire possible and permissible in this democracy of ours was broad, weak domestic comedy. That's why I married off Li'l Abner and began to concentrate on him again. I was absolutely sure that to keep on with political satire—with things like Shmoos—would be to commit suicide."

The strip also pulsed with beautiful women. (For which, in their often gratuitous appearances—they often have nothing to do with the action—Capp was criticized as much as praised.) There was the fetching Moonbeam McSwine, who prefers the company of hogs to men (she naps in Hamfat Gooch's hogpen), gorgeous, lazy, wallowing happily in the mud, trying to ensnare Abner with her buxom charms. ("Anyone who likes small bosoms," Capp once pronounced, "let 'em read *Orphan Annie*.") There was the luscious Stupefyin' Jones, whose irresistible figure stupefies "all red-blooded men." And Fantasia Brown. And Cave Gal. And Tenderleif Erikson,

the sloe-eyed, big-breasted Viking beauty ("After 947 years on ice - Ay need hoosband, by yimminy!! Ay bane single long enough!!") who almost caught Li'l Abner one Sadie Hawkin's Day. And the wildly savage Wolf Gal, who, with her feral lewdness, always ran that race and whose costume, a light tunic with only one shoulder strap and a half open miniskirt, drew the wrath of national Mother's Clubs, especially since a Philadelphia high school chose her as their class symbol, and Al had to add a strap and sew up the sides of the skirt. Nancy O. was a lovely mysterious creature who appeared in the strip (we never saw her face) with whom Abner fell hopelessly in love. A contest was held in 1950 to find "the sweetest face in America," to give her one from photographs sent in of real people.

Daisy Mae Scraggs is, of course, the paragon of them all—beautiful, stupid, chaste, and half-naked: a character with a perfect figure, barometer of popular male taste at any given time, modeled, not as many think, on Marilyn Monroe, but, initially, or so Capp once pointed out, after a secretary in the Associated Press

THAR!-MAH FACE IS WASHED CLEAN!-GOSH!-AH IS **HOMELY!!**

office in New York, then on Silent Screen star Barbara LaMarr. "She may be forgotten now," said Capp, "but when Barbara LaMarr inhaled, boys became men." At yet another time, Capp indicated that Daisy had been modeled on English actress Madeline Carroll, whose most famous movie was Alfred Hitchcock's *The 39 Steps*, and later, he said, Veronica Lake. In 1944 he admitted giving Daisy Mae a resemblance to Lois Eastman, a beautiful opera singer. This was typical Capp. He wasn't lying about a model: he simply made things up, often gave versions of stories—or variations of things—for fun. I'm convinced Daisy Mae was all of those women. Then again, maybe none of them. That was the way Al was, a prankster. Often he was truly amazed, even shocked, that people believed, or did not believe, what he had uttered.

The satirist, by definition, ridicules in order to correct. It was Capp's métier and gave a didactic, even if often hamhanded, twist to his work. There were always some degree of satire at one level or other operating in the strip. And topical buffoonery. And cameo appearances of a kind. Adorable Jones was, for example, a dead ringer for Churchill. Romeo Scragg, one of the Scragg Brothers, looked exactly like John Barrymore. Rockewell P. Squeezeblood ran the cartoonist's syndicate. He came up with names like J. P. Gorganfeller for a millionaire and Southbrook Juggler for a columnist. Bet-a-Million Bashby looked like Benito Mussolini. Adam Lazonga resembled George Bernard Shaw. Marryin' Sam was the spitting image of Fiorello LaGuardia, who, it may be remembered, was once known for reading the comics over the radio to New Yorkers during a newspaper strike. And Orson Waggon is a revoltingly over-confident boy who, at the age of twelve, in spite of his freckles, loud jackets, and big bum, has already written the world's greatest symphony, a novel, and plans to write, direct and star in a radio play.

Drusilla Pearson satirized real-life counterpart Drew Pearson. Earthquake McGoon was surely modeled on the famous wrestler Man Mountain Dean. Silent Yokum was a take-off on the dark-bearded Smith Brothers on the cough drop box. Ezio the Pincher, mocking Ezio Pinza, the Pavarotti of his day, was a wizened little pickpocket who thieved the jewelry of opera-goers; and J. Freud Muggs, named after a TV chimp, is a fat, balding Jewish psychiatrist ("Describe the wictim— oops!—I minn, the hobject of your affections," he asks Prudence Pimpleton, Fosdick's ugly fiancee, who tells him she's in love). In one strip, Al Capp himself appears as Al De Capitate, the "Cecil B. DeMille of the guillotine," a nasty old creep of an executioner. In another, an astrologer appears named Al Capricorn.

And there was of course everybody's favorite, the stalwart detective Fearless Fosdick, sporting sundry bullet holes ("Fortunately, these are merely flesh wounds"). He was a straight arrow, the perfect fool, the classic spoof of Dick Tracy, popular hero of Chester Gould (mocked as wispy little "Lester Gooch" in Capp's strip). Annoyingly incorruptible, cripplingly obedient to authority, a cheapskate, earnest, always ravenously hungry—he craves steak and is always raiding Miss Prudence Pimpleton's refrigerator—Fosdick, whose hometown is Honesty, Indiana, is Li'l Abner's perpetual "ideel."

Racial stereotypes abound. It didn't bother Capp, nor apparently anyone else. Those were different times. Indians, when not savage, are mean-spirited little tricksters. Jewish lawyers are venal and banana-nosed. Russians are untruthful. Blacks don't even appear. Well, maybe one or two do in a token way. Southern rednecks are slobs, aimless dunces. In South America, Li'l Abner meets Don Slumberto and other lazy oafs. Frank Nutsy, based on mobster Frank Nitti, Al Capone's successor, is a greaseball of a gangster, and his hoods a bunch of Italian morons called the "Unteachables." Isn't some sort of Malthusian comment also being made with the hideously homely J. P. McFruitfuls, who have forty or so kids? And places with unsubtle names like Lower Slobbovia, teeming with grim and incompetent yahoos like the devious Quentin Rasputinreynolds—war correspondent for the Slobiviated Press—and creatures like Nogudniks give no small idea of, and very little doubt about, Capp's feelings for the Soviet Union and anyone whom he felt soft on or sympathetic to it.

"I don't like *Li'l Abner* for the good people in it. I like it for the bad ones. The monsters," said Capp. It's an attitude many shared. Al Capp's standing offer of a prize for the "most gruesome" face for Lena the Hyena (who,

incidentally, came from Lower Slobbovia) elicited one million replies. Basil Wolverton, incidentetally, who became one of the more significant comic book artist in later days, was the winner of the "Lena the Hyena" contst, with a stunningly repulsive portrait. Can comic strips still be this powerful? When Dagwood and Blondie couldn't decide on a name for their second child, over 400,000 readers wrote in with suggestions. Or so it is said. In fact, King Features tried a number of these phony scams as a rather shameless attempt to boost cir-

culation, and this was a good example of their Barnumism. Dagwood was popular, but not as fulsome as Hearst's propaganda.

Capp loved words and invented many of them: "druthers," "hogwash!" "natcherly," "namely" (no, he didn't make that word up, but thought of it as his own adverb). Like George Herriman and Rube Goldberg and the other childhood heroes of his who did the comic strips, Capp was not only a cartoonist, but a writer. "No artist who can write should avoid words; no author who can draw should avoid drawing," Capp told Catalina Kitty Meyer in an interview. "That's what a cartoonist can do and so we've always been looked down upon because we have one extra talent." Just as Popeye's creator, E. C. Segar gave us words like "Jeep," "Goon" and "Wimpy," Capp gave us phrases that became over the years part of the American lingo: "as any fool can plainly see," "writ by hand," "oh, happy day," "amoozin' but confoozin'," "there's less to this than meets the eye," "It Hain't Necessarily Moe" (the actual name of a huge black-bearded peckerwood), and no end of exclamations like "sob," "gulp" and "aargh." He of course gave us the term "Sadie Hawkin's Day," as well as the popular occasion itself, usually November 18, but many times it fell when Capp wanted it to fall. Thousands of such races are still popularly run by colleges, fraternities—or sororities—country clubs, and, as Capp said in 1969, "just gangs of desperate girls." (The actual concept of women chasing men for marriage is not strictly new. Many Old World countries have a kind of Sadie Hawkin's Day. In France, for instance, it is St. Catherine's Day.)

Capp dared to be innovative. "The adventure-comic strips of the period," as Updike accurately observed, "presented a wooden superman—Mandrake the Magician, the Phantom, Smilin' Jack, Joe Palooka—left over from a simpler time, an era of stark laborious myths and inflexible draughtsmanship. Capp, with his rollicking abundance of fanciful grotesques and topical allusions, broke this mold...." And he did so in a unique way. His cartoons mixed caricature with intensive regional and cultural realism. Underneath is social seriousness, if not solemnity, and, if it's not an oxymoron, almost Marxist humor. There was great rural poverty in the 1930s, and even very early one of Capp's satirical themes was the relationship between the migrant picker and his labor bosses. "The characters of Li'l Abner live in a world of clear-cut class and power structure, in which the energetic neurotics run everybody else by dint of brass, guile, crime, and paranoia," writes Rouel Denney, who, in The Revolt against Naturalism, sees Capp as a naturalist. "The strip has never lost its hurt, serious tone of concern with inequality of social opportunity, no matter how much the poor and the sick are made to triumph in the end."

Comic strips go back 3,000 years. Egyptians were amused by cartoons of animals, drawn, copied, and circulated on limestone flakes and papyrus. In the 1st century BC tabulae with satirical cartoons were immensely popular in Rome. Comic strips owe their immediate origin to capitalist competition—specifically, the newspaper feud between W. R. Hearst and Joseph Pulitzer in New York in the 1890s. Cartoons, first syndicated in 1913 by Moses Keonigsberg, were used to attract circulation. They were in fact originally addressed to children—Outcault's *The Yellow Kid* was the very first strip—and, as Heinz Politzer observes, "since educators at the beginning of the century looked on children as small, stupid, and rough adults, the producers of the comics chose the sensational, the luridly fantastic, and the exotic—cruelty with a happy ending. And this, in the main, still remains the case." In the '30s, Al had seen prophetically that the golden age of American illustration was coming to an end, that photography was taking over, along with radio and, of course, comics. By pointing this out to magazine illustrator Raeburn Van Buren, he convinced him in 1936 to do the drawings for *Abbie an' Slats*, which became a huge success. It was Capp's idea and he wrote the entire story line of the strip until its demise in 1971. He had a very strong grasp, until toward the end of his life, not only about cartoons but about our culture. He was an inveterate newspaper reader, listened to talk-shows, and often called in with opinions.

Although most would acknowledge that comic strips are a lowbrow art form—a fact that has often made Al Capp self-conscious and often defensive—he saw *Li'l Abner* as a paragon of that world. At 61, Capp, interestingly enough, began painting, working with acrylics and borrowing stylistically from his own strips, almost as if to justify them or, what seemed to be in a larger sense always on his mind, to prove himself worthy, and who can say, maybe even exploit the movement to advantage. Like Roy Lichtenstein, Capp's work meets the gimmicky, popular, and glamorous definition of the kind of pop-art that was popular at the time. Al of course hated the term and no doubt saw it as reductionistic. He despised critics, loathed jargon, and was suspicious of "schools." He explained, simply, that he wanted to bring the comic strip "out of the closet," to "demonstrate that your daily newspaper's comic page gives you as many respectable works of art... as all the galleries in town." It was always his belief that cartoonists were neglected. "A work of art is a work of art, regardless of form, size, or material," Capp said in an interview for an exhibition of his works at the New York Cultural Center in 1970. "People have been brainwashed into thinking that if it appears in a comic strip and in your daily newspaper, and done with pen and ink, it is a contemptible trifle, it isn't art. That is self-swindling snobbishness."

William Bolitho in his essay "Comic Strip" from *Camera Obscura* (1930) points out that "trivialities" compose the real originality and flavor of countries and finds American comic strips highly valuable. "Nations," he writes, "are almost always slightly ashamed of their truly admirable idiosyncrasies," among which he numbers cartoons. To Bolitho, cartoons are "as special and interesting at least as Egyptian hieroglyphics." In them he finds "the creation of a world, true only to its own laws, where humanity may escape and disport itself, away from the other imposed reality." He sees the art as sociologically diagnostic. "As a mere matter of philosophic philology, in the countless balloons that float daily from the grotesque mouths of these marionettes (the Gothic carvings of our days) there is registered the most indisputably authentic anthology of our ways of speech, our very jokes.... Pickwick started notoriously as a sort of celestial comic strip."

With an almost roosterish defensiveness that would become a trademark, especially later, in the relentlessly nagging and cross-grained contentiousness of his politics, Al Capp, like Bolitho, considered the American comic strip to be "as unique, as vigorous and as precious an art as American jazz" and regretted "that those with the gift of finding humor in living should be treated as second class artists by art critics." He singles out for example the "grace" of *Steve Canyon*. (Milton Caniff actually regarded the adventures of *Steve Canyon* as a picaresque novel.) Capp had the working-man's suspicion of intellectuals. He was scornful of modern art in general and hated abstract art, which he breezily—and, no doubt, competitively—dismissed, without a thought to philistinism, as "the product of the untalented, sold by the unprincipled to the totally bewildered." In defense of his own art, he could sometimes become ludicrous. "The genuine art today," Capp said, "is the art of the auto ads, fashion magazines and comic strips." We tend to repeat what we want to believe to reinforce what we fear to deny. It was almost as if the importunate need to so insist on what he felt diminished his argument. Needless to say, it is a debate that will be around for a long time. "Capp has a story but has to tell it," as critic Kenneth Tynan remarked, "on a mass-circulation scale, which means there are limits to the amount of intellectual contraband [he] can smuggle into print."

Capp soon had everything he wanted. He was literary, and he was lionized. *Life* magazine featured him on its cover for March 31, 1952. He appeared on the covers of *Time* and *Newsweek* and was profiled by *The New*

Yorker. He put out records, marketed merchandise, sold books and compilations. There were also his paintings. He had advertising contracts with Wildroot Cream-Oil hair tonic and Cream of Wheat. The musical comedy, *Li'l Abner*, based on his characters (book by Norman Panama and Melvin Frank), opened on November 15, 1956 at the St. James Theatre in New York, after engagements in Washington, Philadelphia, and Boston. For eight years he supplied the storyline for *Abbie an' Slats*. At various points he was a columnist for the Daily News Syndicate and became a regular syndicated radio commentator. He once even co-hosted the Mike Douglas TV show for a week, inviting on Lester Maddox, ex-Governor of Georgia, whom he had once angrily seen mocked and vilified on the Dick Cavett Show by Cavett, Truman Capote, and black actor, Jim Brown.

Among his close friends he numbered Igor Cassini, Hugh Hefner, Bernie Cornfeld, William F. Buckley, Art Buchwald, Orson Welles, Ross Perot, whom he met on an airplane over Texas one day—and with whom he once toyed with brokering a deal, though nothing came of it—and, during the latter part of his life, especially the early 1970s, President Richard M. Nixon and Vice-President Spiro T. Agnew.

Curiously, especially for those who recall only the Capp of later years, *Li'l Abner* was at first the vehicle for liberal views. Capp railed at the power of money, mocked Congress and the White House, and lampooned capitalists. (It's my belief that the comic strip *Li'l Abner* is one long fable about greed, of which sex is but one variation.) The far "right" to him was suspect. He dismissed with scornful laughter fat, graft-ridden reactionaries like J. Roaringham Fatback; Mr. Dumpington Van Lump, the little oaflet millionaire ("I own the building. In fact, as I recall-I own the whole block!") who covets Daisy Mae and who whacks his slavish minions with an umbrella to relieve his feelings, and thundering General Bullmoose, the richest man in the world (his motto: "What's good for General Bullmoose is good for the USA"), a loud, ruthless tycoon as bad as Commodore Vanderbilt or Daddy Warbucks, whose "ward," Appassionata von Climax, in the musical comedy based on the strip, it may be recalled, tries by her sexual wiles to inveigle out of Li'l Abner his secret for Yokumberry tonic. Mr. Fangbottom, a capitalist of measureless greed, might have stepped out of *Mother Jones* or an inflammatory *New Masses* cartoon.

Ironically, at least in the light of his later politics, the pro-Republican *Pittsburgh Press* protested that Al's pompous, reactionary politico, Sen. Jack S. Phogbound, was a calculated libel on the reputation of the US Senate. (Congress? Corrupt? What better proof of what the happy fifties were like?) Many outraged readers back then often wrote and complained that Capp's cartoons

Who's Who in Pork ®

J. Roaringham Fatback: "King of Pork". Born in Hammond, Indiana. Educated at **Sow Western** University. Merged his tiny **FCC** *(Fatback's Chops and Cutlets)* with **IBCo.** *(International Bacon)* and became most prominent figure in the world of Swine. Resides on Pork Ave., New York — and summers at **Newpork, Rhode Island.** His fire and sparkle have always

Fatback

were setting back American morals and undermining the Constitution itself. Capp was undaunted, staying bravely on track, caricaturing whomever he wanted to and satirically turning the lights up on corruption. Look closely. Most of the subjects of the dark side of the fifties—fear of the bomb, McCarthyism, anxieties about the "organization man" losing his soul, the rebellion of the Beat counterculture, even the unhappiness of many middle-class American women—Capp handled in one way or another in his strip. He mocked everything, kicking ass when he needed to and in a way that can't have been anything but fun. He had the power to release national derision. He even campaigned for Stevenson and Kennedy. "Capp is decidedly oracular," wrote Arthur Asa Berger in *Li'l Abner, A Study in American Satire*. "He speaks out of both sides of his mouth at once, though in real life he is considered a liberal."

Al Capp, in defense of the common man, espoused many a cause. On his own, he mounted campaigns against zoot suits, big business, Southern congressman, outdoor advertising signs. In one comic strip

sequence, much to the great grief of the Outdoor Advertising Association who publicly admonished the cartoonist, Li'l Abner and Daisy Mae go on a sight-seeing trip and Abner tears down a hundred and fifty unsightly billboards along a stretch of otherwise scenic highway. "Gosh!!" cries Daisy Mae afterward, "Hain't America a bootiful country—it's even more bootiful than billboards advertising pork, beans, girdles, shoes, cheese, an' crackers!!" Capp loved tweaking noses. And occasionally it got him into scrapes. Sinatra fans once became furious at him for a series in which an unmistakable prototype of pencil-thin Frankie Boy—Li'l Abner, in fact—was shown wasting away and eventually dying of malnutrition. (One bobby-soxer promised to devote the rest of her life to not reading *Li'l Abner*.) Another time, Al received a long-distance call from a Mr. Marsh advising him his wife found no humor in Capp's parody entitled "Gone Wif the Wind," threatening him with legal penalties for infringement on Mrs. Marsh's book amounting to $1 for every copy of every paper in which the parody had so far appeared," $75,000,000 as of that day, and Mammy Yokum made an obliging and immediate two-panel apology and the incident was forgotten. Mr. Marsh, it turns out, was Margaret Mitchell's husband.

A serious change, however, came over Capp sometime in the sixties. He was restless and unfulfilled. He wanted to go to England and write. He was having trouble with his family, whom he considered selfish, especially his kids whom he felt ignored him and wanted only his money. Private letters he wrote at this time are filled with accusations. *Pogo* and *Doonesbury* were now the popular strips. Authority was being questioned everywhere, and discipline was breaking down. So he turned to the right and became conservative—some would say

negative, a cartoon almost like his own General
Bullmoose, who looked on Herbert Hoover as a dangerous radical. He lost patience with the "left," became
abrasive, and was soon beginning to alienate almost
everybody. The "frog-voiced, razor-witted Daumier of
Dogpatch," as *Time* once described him, now became
shrill and bleating and cruel. He could mock with exper-
tise. He sounded at times truly unappeasable. He created in his comic strip, bitterly to mock it, a radical political group called S.W.I.N.E. ("Students Wildly Indignant
Against Nearly Everything") who gain power when a
mysterious gas incapacitates everyone who has washed
during the previous 48 hours. A folk singer, Joanic
Phoanie, is mocked, who performs for starving orphans
before returning to her limousine to eat caviar. (Joan
Bacz took him to court.) During this period, his strip's
often (still) extremely funny solution to student unrest at
Harvard was to have the Mafia take over.

Capp saw all hippies as layabouts and slobs. He hated their hairiness. (Would anyone be surprised to learn that all through later life he himself was irrationally terrified about going bald?) He despised what he considered their false ideals and baited them. He believed in work. Laziness especially incensed him. (The satire is not lost on us when, after he gets married, Li'l Abner himself lands a job as a mattress-tester, sleeping comfortably from 6 a.m. to 6 p.m.—with just enough time to eat lunch!—on his "Little Wonder Mattress.") Did Capp perhaps feel threatened by the incapacitating immobility, or ultimate stasis, a wooden leg implied, fighting in silent anger against that easy, demeaning option always open to paraplegics? Many characters in *Li'l Abner* are partial to such adjectives as "repulsive," "ugly," "miserable," "loathsome," and "revolting." But whereas the words once carried a patina of humor, now they were barbed. Capp seemed to make no distinctions between hippies and students and young people in general. Weren't they all the same? He berated Peace Corps volunteers for going abroad with help when he insisted we needed it here at

home. (He was also saying at the same time America was in fine shape.) An argument could easily be made that he came to resent youth itself, suspect *anybody* young of guile. In any case, as art historian Frank Whitford pointed out in 1975, "Capp has become the William F. Buckley of the drawing board."

"For some 30 years," Capp explained to one interviewer in 1975, "I was a believing liberal. I hailed liberal causes, jeered at reactionaries.... Reams of words appeared about my fearlessness. About ten years ago I became increasingly worried about the takeover of American thought by reckless, often balmy, liberals. Their attitude, and the attitude of their press, was reminiscent of Goebbles and his press.... When I began to mock the liberals, there came a deluge of hate mail which never ended. Instantly, my radio commentary show was ended, my TV show, which would have started in 56 stations, never begun. I was never again asked as a guest on the air. Editorials in magazines and newspapers, which less than a year before were calling me the great comic

historian of our time, now denounced me as a bitter fascist. That reaction was painful, of course. Everyone likes to be liked. It convinced me, however, that anyone who fears American fascism should be grateful for the bumblers of Watergate and had damn well now better look to the left."

At one point, Capp even considered running for the U.S. Senate in Massachusetts against Teddy Kennedy, claiming he could generate enough Texas money "to match Kennedy buck for buck." It may simply have been part of an elaborate joke, but he did switch his party affiliation, did join the Republican party, and did give several speeches, only to find himself, gratefully, in my opinion, thwarted by an odd Massachusetts law that held a voter switching parties is prohibited from running for public office the following year.

Instead, he took up lecturing, getting as much as $5,000 an appearance. Going from college to college, in the '60s almost always the "enemy camp," he scolded students for their sloth and muddled thinking, berated radicals as communists, and ridiculed young liberals, some would say, not so much for the opinions they held as for merely holding them. ("The opinions of eighteen year olds are valuable on things they know something about, such as puberty and hubcaps, but nothing else," sneered Capp.) It brought him the kind of notoriety he wasn't sure was welcome or should be eschewed, for Capp both loved and hated attention, was a private man and yet a public figure. I think he never expected fame on that scale, or at least fame along those lines, though he felt obliged, at times smugly, at times perhaps honestly, to try meeting it head on. The satirist behind the drawing board was suddenly a public figure. There was a cocky aggression that exacerbated his black, disapproving persona and seemed to make dogma out of chance remarks. The kind of simpering cynicism that mocked and belittled in comic strip blocks became a plague of opposition at the lectern.

He had a false nervous laugh. He was loud, with a self-congratulating chortle that seemed the epitome of smugness. When he talked, his hands, with thumbs out, churned and rotated incessantly. He chewed and hummed through long pauses, biting the air contumaciously, as he flicked ashes off a wagging omnipresent cigarette in any and every direction. He had a folksy, outdated reliance on words like "damfool" and "helluva note." According to writer Richard Woodley, even his smile seemed baleful. "When he smiled, his eyebrows sloped precipitously down, closing his eyes while his mobile mouth, as if in reaction to a downward punch from his nose, arced upward and remains open." He could boom with dark anger, crucify with exaggeration, brutally oversimplify, become wildly illogical, be certainly unfair or unkind, and then be just as often funny—and all of this often in once sentence. He was his own favorite audience.

What insecurities were his, not unrelated perhaps to his meagre formal education, were arguably reflected in the flashy clothes he seemed to need; in his pronounced Anglophilia; in the calling cards he kept in bountiful supply, bearing, like his personal stationery, not only his name but the image of Li'l Abner; in the self-aggrandizement-by-association he felt by being in the company of presidents; in the flashy brand-new Cadillac convertibles with eye-catching colors he drove with the words "Al Capp" stylishly reproduced in the script with which he signed his comic strips, painted on the door.

Al Capp loved the Question and Answer forum. He would request groups to have index cards printed: "Al Capp Is An Expert On Nothing But Has Opinions On Everything. What Is Your Question?" which were distributed to his audience ahead of time. It is messianic form, to be sure. He would then gather the cards and, sitting alone in his hotel room hours before the lecture, compose witty replies. All are revealing. Most are funny. Many are silly. Some are vain. And a lot of them seem positively self-deluded. A few examples follow:

Q: Does anyone know anything about ABM, or is it just that the majority of the public is apathetic?
A: I made up my mind on one sure-fire rule. If Teddy Kennedy is for anything, I'm agin it.

Q: Are the characters you portray ever a reflection of yourself?
A: All are—chastity of Daisy Mae, naiveté of Li'l Abner.

Q: Are you for or against euthanasia?
A: For whom? Clarify.

Q. Why are you such a harsh and cruel critic?
A: If you want a gentle critic, go to your mother.

Q: What inspired you as an artist to write a comic strip on hillbillies?
A: Money.

Q: Are you familiar with the advantages of the see-through blouse?
A: There are two.

Q: We hear a lot about the generational gap. What are your thoughts on this subject?
A: Not wide enuff.

(A last example, part megalomanical, part paranoid, reveals, as do many, a bitterness perhaps long boiling in Capp.)

Q: Why haven't you won the Nobel Prize?
A: Anti-Semitism.

He was ferociously sexist, bigoted, bitter, anti-intellectual, many would say, hopelessly antediluvian, and at the end, right wing in an almost comic or cartoon way. (Nixon cultivated his friendship and Agnew wrote to him quite often.) A lot of it was a persona he invented and flaunted, nothing more. It is quite often the artist's temptation. Half the time, I'm convinced, he was performing for himself. But it filled him with a hateful energy that focused not only on his subject but on the credulous audience that perhaps—and stupidly, Capp might have felt—couldn't see that. He often got carried away, caught up in rhetoric, even charmed by the whirlwind of his own polemics. He had a terrible need to be a quipster, a nagging need to know more than anyone else. I've listened to many of these tapes, which are almost embarrassing in the baldly confrontational and name-calling approach he took, completely out of sync with any kind of academic forum. He was often consumed, I feel, by the newness of, the very mode of communication, standing up before people, orating, just as Charles Dickens had been in the late, almost apoplectic readings that had cost that novelist his life. Capp began to believe his right wing pronouncements. Big money was coming in from political groups, the D.A.R., the Elks, all back-slapping him and urging him on.

Although he had many followers and drew much laughter and applause, he was more often booed by the students, the very kind from Emerson College he saw every day—and began to resent—outside on the street in front of his studio, among the "artiest" in the country. Developing a fortress mentality, he called himself a "steam valve for Nixon and Agnew." Presidents not only impressed him ("...Truman told me..." "...as I got to know President Eisenhower...") but co-opted him. Now he was going to the White House and was proud of it. He loved controversy, saying things like, "What should we do in Vietnam? I say shoot back," and "The Peace Corps to me is a man in a corner saloon saying drinks for everybody, on me, while his own children are home crying for milk."

He thought blacks whined. "I know hunger. There isn't any real hunger in the country any more. With food so cheap, anybody can buy enough to survive, and even keep healthy. We should quit giving handouts. That's just treating people as inferiors. You have to believe that black people are just as capable of making it as we are. Let them clean up their own ghettos. I grew up in a Jewish ghetto and loved it. I *liked* being with my own kind. I know what it is to be imprisoned—by a wooden leg. I can't run, but I don't go around hating mechanical contrivances because this leg was lopped off by a trolley car when I was nine. For chrissake, every man has his black skin, every man has his wooden leg." And welfare mothers particularly disgusted him. "Anyone who can walk to the welfare office can walk to work." "Unwed mothers must be capable of some other form of labor." Chastity belts, he said, were his solution for the unwed-mother-on-welfare problem, observing, "and the welfare department would keep the key."

In 1971, he wrote—or compiled—*The Hardhat's Bedtime Story Book*, a collection of feuilletonistic essays, more than fifty of them, virtually all ridiculing liberals as fools and phonies. They are more silly than bitter, though remarkably acrimonious they are puerile to a fault, and singularly artless. It's not so much embarrassing that a man of Capp's stature would actually bother to sit down to write such childish (and humorless) stuff, but that someone of his age could get so angry and out of control about—would spend time on—such trivia. He tilts against a whole row of windmills: Ho Chi Swine; earnest Jane Porna, a movie star sympathetic to Vietcong; Senator Eugene McArtsy-Craftsy; Senator George McGrovel ("...groveling at the feet of the minuscule minority of the untoilet-trained on our campuses..."); Miss Ann Yewly Fruitful, mother of nine and national chairman of MUMs (Militant Unwed Mothers); actor Paul Newleft; even Harvbaked, the Ivy League university that coddles students. This is the man at his shrillest.

Capp was an enigma, an amalgam of contradictions. His laugh was both hearty and hateful. He had an innocent, almost naive side that wanted to be loved, according to his friends a side tempered by its other half, cunning, brilliant, shrewd, and arrogant. ("It was a big relief to all his friends when Al realized he no longer needed to tell people how good he was," said the otherwise characteristically gentle Milton Caniff.) Much in Capp was misanthropic. Yet he had millions of readers and huge fans. There were many interruptions in public, at dinner, on the street. "So you're Al Capp?" "Are you still alive?" which he met with scorn and obloquy. And yet he could treat audiences of thousands with tenderness. He deliberately signed his checks in an illegible paraph, so people wouldn't save them as autographs. And yet he slavishly sought their approval and agreement. He was not religious but said, "The older I get, the more American and the more Jewish I feel." As to his lecturing, how could public occasions, so embarrassing to him early in life, mean so much to him later on? Was he trying to kill that devil? Or himself? Why did he like students to be square, solid and polite—types that bored him? Types he never drew? Or despise young people as know-it-alls, when, in his lectures he was dining-out quite evidently on the same menu?

And while many of the themes in his cartoons were reflected in his personal essays and writing, as well as in his lectures—the pain and embarrassment of disfigurement; contrast between justice and reason in art and the injustice and disorder of life; greed and being bilked; the anxieties of fame; girls and sex, especially—where in his comic strip a relatively light, even if barbed levity was maintained, with humor relieving the blackness, in real life it simply wasn't so. In a strict sense, Capp's art *processed* his life, rolling it over in terms of and through exaggeration, which may have kept him sane but at the same time left him looking sourly and unhappily at a life that reflected nothing like the same order and over which he had comparatively much less control.

What informed his bitterness? Did he cultivate and Ahabian hatred ("I'd strike the sun if it insulted me," cried the antihero of *Moby-Dick*) for everything he felt robbed of in his childhood accident? Why was he so unforgiving to students? What did he see when he saw them: opportunities, leisure, the degrees he himself never had? Did he resent aging? Was it a bile borne of personal resentment? An extension of the anger he often felt at his own children? "Princeton has sunk to a moral level only a chimpanzee can live with." "President Nixon showed angelic restraint when he called students bums." He wasn't any kinder to teachers. "Colleges today are filled with Fagin professors who don't teach.... They just corrupt." "Why do students cause so much trouble today?" he asked. "Because they have thirteen billion dollars to spend. Never before has it been so profitable

to kiss the ass of the kids. Half the records they go out and buy today are 'hate America' records." It wasn't he who had changed, of course. It was the sanctimonious, unpatriotic, placard-carrying know-it-alls who had. "*Our* generation did great things. We are the first generation that ever said we *are* our brother's keeper. *Our* generation produced Jonas Salk and Albert Schweitzer. We beat Hitler and survived Joe McCarthy."

He called humanitarians "pests" and applauded students "motivated by avarice" as being more honest and better for the country. He wasn't averse to violence. "The real Kent State martyrs were the kids in uniforms," he said. And for any protesters driven over and killed, their parents "could get George Jessel to deliver the eulogy." It was as if he could only make a point by exaggeration. The caricatures of his comic strip became distortions in his repartee. He could also be crude. His favorite Q & A cards, in fact, were sexual, not political. "You show me a student who's concerned about a breakdown of morals, and I'll show you a guy who's not getting any action." "What do I think about a two o'clock Saturday night curfew? I say, if you can't score by two o'clock...." It seems only sad in echo, for, if any one picture emerges from Al Capp's memoirs, it's the image of himself as a young and alienated teenager, a lost boy who craved normalcy, envied Yalies, never scored, but double-bouncing on a wooden peg, crow-hopped gimpily away from any girl he saw for feeling himself a freak.

The last ten years of Capp's life were bitter, resentful, and, coincident with a slowly emerging darker side, controversial. The predominant reason for much of his decline, and the cause of his becoming something of a pariah and then a recluse, happened in 1972, when at the University of Wisconsin, he was accused of "attempted adultery"—a crime in that state—with a twenty year old college student, identified only as Mrs. H. It turns out this wasn't the first sexual offense. One account goes back to the fifties. He had auditioned Grace Kelly for the role of Daisy Mae in the Broadway musical. Jeannie Sakol and Caroline Latham in *About Grace: An Intimate Notebook* write, "She arrived at his office alone, when he took advantage of the situation to sexually molest her. She fought him off and managed to escape in tears with her dress torn. Although tempted to bring charges against him, she decided it would reflect badly on her own reputation." He had also apparently committed similar sexual offenses, repeatedly, on a lecture tour at the University of Alabama back in 1968. A shocking Jack Anderson exposé in a column

recounting those escapades in detail, sexual propositions to coeds, four of them in the course of a day and a half, went on to explain how Capp, after receiving a telephone call from Anderson, immediately boarded a plane in Boston and flew down to Washington to discuss the matter, insufficiently, according to Anderson, who proceeded to report the ambiguity of Capp's repeated non-denial

("I have never become involved with any student") and to describe how in Wisconsin he had been literally evicted from the state, ordered out, bag and baggage, deported like an illegal alien. It would soon become a national scandal.

Al appeared less contrite than angered over the Wisconsin incident, irked, it seemed, that something like this could happen to him. From his explanations, he felt too much had been made of nothing. Why was everyone so upset? He warranted a bit of entitlement, he felt, like most people who move affairs, at least assumed it, and I think considered himself somewhat immune to the laws of common men. He tended to dislike authority. In his comic strip, he rather unflinchingly took great chances with libel, as satirists tend to do, and was always more or less tweaking someone's nose, although as E. J. Kahn, Jr. in his *New Yorker* "profile" of 1946 pointed out, "Capp himself rarely has any trouble with the police."

Anderson's column, "Capp Escorted off Campus," which many newspapers tactfully suppressed, was run on May 4, 1971 in the Boston *Phoenix*. Based on interviews and affidavits, it explains how Capp arrived in Tuscaloosa on February 11, 1968 to make a speech at the university's annual arts festival. At the Stafford Hotel where he was staying, Al Capp made "forceful advances" on four separate occasions to four different coeds—all on innocent missions, one delivering a yearbook he had requested, another whose job it was to greet visiting speakers, another was a reporter, etc.—"exposed himself" to them and "made suggestive comments." By next morning, reports of each of the incidents had reached the administration, including Dr. Frank Rose, university president, who confronted him. Al Capp was summarily ordered to leave Tuscaloosa. President Rose personally

followed Capp's car to the town line. "He was asked to get out and did get out and went to Birmingham," Anderson reported he was told by college security director Col. Beverly Lee. "The young women were not physically harmed and we felt that the publicity and notoriety should be avoided," said Dean of Women, Sarah Healy, of the University of Alabama.

And now there was Wisconsin. What happened there has never been made fully clear. Versions and rumors abounded. In a snide piece, the October 1971 issue of *National Lampoon* referred to the act of "sodomy," Capp in fact was officially the subject of three charges: sodomy, attempted adultery, as well as indecent exposure. Capp said that Mrs. H. had visited him prior to one of his lectures, as she was one of the students with an "Ask Al Capp" card. He said she was "left-wing" and called her a "do-gooder determined to remake me." He claims it was she who brought up the subject of sex, boasted how she and her husband had a "special arrangement." Capp defensively quoted her as saying, "My husband had certain sexual difficulties, but I overcame them," and "He is an apt pupil." At one point, after their meeting, she went to meet her husband in the lobby when he had come to pick her up prior to the lecture. According to Capp, her husband seemed angry and threatened Capp, who claimed he didn't know why. Capp implies he'd have met that threat, but for his wooden leg. Immediately after the lecture Capp left Wisconsin.

What exactly had happened? Had the woman set out to ensnare Capp sexually? Politically? Had she been wired, wearing a hidden mike? Did everybody in the lecture hall hear his sexual overtures over a PA system, as one report had it? In a detailed column, in any case, columnist Jack Anderson and an assistant who had earlier interviewed Capp, Brit Hulme ("a fag," Capp said) blew the whistle in the press.

Capp, meanwhile, having long endeared himself to the White House, beginning in March 1971, by having taken the podium at the annual convention of the National Association of Broadcasters and castigating the three major television networks as well as Tom Wicker, the liberal columnist of the *Times*, for what he claimed was their bias against Nixon, desperately now looked to Washington for help. We now know that Nixon got Charles Colson to go to Wisconsin to try to fix the case by pressuring Lawrence W. Durning, the Eau Claire district attorney at the time. Durning refused to play ball.

The story was out. Lawyer Edward Bennett Williams was hired to defend Capp. Judge Elijah Adlow released Capp in personal recognizance after

Detective Sergeant Herbert Lynch asked for a continuance. A Boston *Phoenix* editorial commented, "If the person involved was somewhat different from Capp—say a black or a freak—he would probably be locked up in the Charles Street jail and rendition hearings would be moving right along." A judgment was rendered. Capp was found guilty in February 1972 of one morals charge—he pleaded guilty to attempted adultery—and fined $500 plus court costs. Two other charges were dropped at the request of the victim, who did not want the case to go to trial. Immediately, hundreds of newspapers dropped *Li'l Abner* from their comics page, including *The Boston Globe*, his hometown paper, as it were. It crushed him. He felt stabbed in the back. The end was at hand.

Ironically, *Confidential*, a salacious, muck-raking magazine of the '50s and '60s ran an article in October

1953, "Al Capp Exposed: The Secret Sex Life," revealing in huge garish headlines, "It Took a New York State Legislative Committee to Reveal the Shocking Fact That a Comic Strip Read by 40 Million People Cunningly Conceals the Type of Lascivious Humor Usually Found Only on Outhouse Walls!" Growing out of Ham Fisher's old, even if refuted, charges as well as a "profile" that E. J. Kahn, Jr. did for *The New Yorker*, where Kahn supposedly vouchsafed the opinion that Capp drew for a secret audience of readers, the article accused Capp of "incursions into ruttishness," of having "a predilection with pornography." Kahn, it turns out, had made the dramatic discovery that Capp had received 25 cents in grade school for each and every "pornographic" drawing he did for various classmates. Several weak examples from Capp's comic strips were run in the articles, showing ambiguous lines and shapes, along with those gonadally-shaped shmoos—which Halston perfume bottles, incidently, highly resemble—as evidence of sexual "suggestiveness." Apparently, the New York Joint Legislative Committee had very little to do back in 1951. It was farcical. But none of it can have pleased Capp.

In 1972, meanwhile, Capp reaped the whirlwind. He pulled in, became hostile towards everyone, even—especially—his family, complaining how they were bilking him of his fortune. He wrote letters saying he didn't want to see them any more. Along with hundreds of newspapers dropping his strip, Cinema General, the entertainment arm of U. S. Steel, who had piled up a large sale for a TV program to be called *The Al Capp Show*, could no longer go with it and let the project fizzle. Whereas he was once quarrelsome on podiums, on television, in print, now he seemed to implode. He lost weight, often sat alone in his rooms, and kept repeating that he wanted to go to England to live, alone, and write, no one knew quite what. John Updike in a poem, "The Shuttle," seemed to sense the burden he bore, the weariness, as he recalled meeting and talking to Al Capp on a virtually empty DC-7, then later at a party:

> one of those Cambridge parties
> where his anti-Ho politics
> were wrong, so wrong
> the left eventually broke his heart
>
> I recalled this to him,
> but did not recall how sleepy
> he looked to me, how tired,
> with his peg-legged limp
>
> and rich man's blue suit
> and Li'l Abner shock of hair.
> He laughed and said to me,
> "And if the plane had crashed,
>
> can't you see the headline?-
> ONLY EIGHT KILLED.
> ONLY EIGHT KILLED: everyone
> would be so relieved!"
>
> Now Al is dead, dead,
> and the shuttle is always crowded.

Al retired in 1977 under a dark cloud, after 43 long years of cartooning, day in and day out. His decision made all the magazines and papers. His last weekday strip appeared on November 5, 1977, his last Sunday color sequence—featuring that peerless detective, Fearless Fosdick—was run on November 13th. He had chosen no successor. "I've tried one or two people, and it was clear that there would be an awful change." He was retiring, he said because of ill health.

"I've had a great shortness of breath for the past five or six years. I really couldn't go on with [the strip]," he said. "I just can't breathe." It was true. He was suffocating. And two years later he died.

Alexander Theroux has taught at Harvard,
MIT, Yale, and the University of Virginia, where he
took his doctorate in 1968. The author of numerous
articles, short stories, essays, novels, plays, and poems,
Theroux is best known as the author of the novels
Darconville's Cat and *An Adultery* and the essay "The
Primary Colors" ("an amazing display of omnidirectional
erudition and an omnivorous poetic instinct,"
according to John Updike). His writing has won
further praise from Anthony Burgess and Saul Bellow.
He resides in West Barnstable, Massachusetts.